Life Still Goes On

Jenna Rose Lowthert

LIFE STILL GOES ON

THE BLOG BOOK OF A MOTHERLESS DAUGHTER

A BOOK OF LOVE, LOSS, AND INSPIRATION TO GO ON.

JENNA ROSE LOWTHERT

DEDICATION

This book is dedicated to my beautiful mother.
Gina Marie Lowthert
October 30, 1964 – May 27, 2013

Happiness is possible.
It is possible because I am happy,
& I am just the same as you.

CONTENTS

ACKNOWLEDGEMENTS

I would like to humbly thank all of those who have supported me through this journey of loss. To my dearest friends who have stuck by my side through it all, and to my family that endured this tragedy as well, I love you all tremendously.

I would like to honor my grandmother, Rosemarie Frio, one of the strongest woman I know; Thank you for showing me the way.

I would also like to extend my profound gratitude to Luis Gouveia- motivator, designer, and believer. Thank you.

Jenna Rose Lowthert

INTRODUCTION

After having to stand up in front of over 300 people and read my 48 year old mother's eulogy at the young age of 24, I realized that life just isn't always what it seems. We will all eventually lose someone we love and care deeply about but losing your mother can be one of the most devastating things in the world. Once she is gone you will see a change in yourself that you never saw coming. Your world will fall apart and you will be given two options. You can get up, get out there, pick up the pieces, put your world back together, and honor your mother by living- or you can sit around and feel sorry for yourself. I think we all could agree that option number one would be what our mothers would want for us.

But that is easier said than done.

After all, the one who is supposed to be here guiding us through this thing they call life, is no longer here. It's a tough pill to swallow, but in the end we have no choice but to realize the plain and simple truth that even through the darkest of days, life does goes on. Life does not stop for anybody, no matter how much we want it to.

In this book you will find stories of the bond between a mother and daughter, life after loss, hope, heartache, grief, and inspiration to go on.

LIFE GOES ON..?

On May 27th, 2013 my beautiful mother, Gina, became my guardian angel. Never in a million years did I think I would become a motherless daughter at the age of 24. But life sometimes throws curve balls at you when you least expect it.

In the middle of my "what seemed like perfect" life I was hit with the biggest curve ball of them all. I will never forget the day that I was told that my mother has stage four non-small cell lung cancer. It all just seemed like a bad nightmare. After all she was only 48 years old. How the hell did this happen?

I knew that when we received her diagnosis the outcome wouldn't be good but we still held onto so much hope. She fought as hard as she could, for as long as she could but just ten short months later, she was gone.

The morning waking up after her passing was one of the worst mornings I'll ever have in my life. That empty feeling, that feeling of knowing I'll never see her again, that feeling that she really is in fact gone. That very same morning was the day I was faced with the two choices I spoke of in the introduction. I chose to pick up the pieces and start to put my world back together.

My mom was one of the greatest people I will ever know. She was so brave, so strong, and so loving. She always put others first and I wanted to be just like her. I know my mom would never want me to lead an unhappy life, so I decided I would now live my life for her. For the years she will miss, I will make up for everything that has been stolen from her.

Almost exactly one year to the date that she passed away, I found my passion for writing. Somehow, some way, I managed to write my very first book titled, "Life Goes On..?" I also started a grief and inspiration blog. The amount of amazing responses I have received since I started on my writing journey is what drives me to keep on going. I hope to inspire others, help others, and ultimately heal others with my own experiences.

THE LOSS OF A MOTHER

"I have cancer" those painful words rolled off my mother's tongue as if to her, she were saying something as simple as "I have ice cream." She was so strong, so brave, and I know that she was that way because she didn't want to see me, my sister, or my father sad, hurt, or scared for her.

A few days after we got that horrible news the four of us sat in a quiet room, waiting for her oncologist to come in to discuss the plan of action.

Nothing in this world could have prepared me for what I was about to hear. Inoperable, terminal, stage four, non-small cell lung cancer that had spread to her bones and lymph nodes.

She was 47 years old. How did that happen? Why her? Why our family? But why anybody?

Never in a million years did I think I would be watching my mother battle cancer, battle chemotherapy, and most importantly fight for her life. But it has to happen to somebody, right?

While I struggled to accept the fact that my mom was going to leave this world sooner than I had ever expected she was off living her life, continuing her normal routines, helping others, inspiring others, and just being the woman everyone always loved and wanted to be around.

I consider every single second that I spent with my mother a blessing, a gift, a chance to say goodbye, even the moments that had caused me so much pain. I was beyond lucky to have been able to be by her side every single moment that time would allow and I sometimes see people choose differently. Some would rather not spend that time with their dying loved one. I believe some can't bear the heartache and some have regrets. But me? I would have never of done differently. Eight months flew by and things seemed to be going okay, until that very last month. I had realized the painful truth that it was beginning of the end. I spent every moment I possibly could with her, by her side, cherishing what little time I subconsciously knew I had left.

I was in denial, I almost didn't want to be there because who wants to see their mother like that? As I watched her moan in pain in a hospital room that I so badly wanted to run out of, as I watched her cry knowing she would be leaving her babies behind, as I listened to her saying her goodbyes in a way that was never really directly saying "goodbye", as I brushed her hair on her final days when clumps fell out into mine and my sisters hands because of the chemotherapy, and as I held her freezing cold hand as the flat line of her heart sounded through the hospital room I realized many would rather have not been there for those moments but for me it would have been far more painful to have never witness those things at all. Far more painful to not have been able to see my mom through the last weeks of her life because I wanted to protect myself from the harsh reality that I was stuck in.

The irony of it all is that while I fought to save her life, I was really fighting to save my own. I never wanted her to know how much losing her would affect my life, change my life, and most importantly ruin my life. I tried to safeguard her from the painful truth of how so very much I would miss her, and I do, with all of my heart, every...single...day.

So here I am, 27 years old, making my way through this world without her guidance. I have come to terms, not with her death, but with this new life I am forced to live and although I would give up everything to have her back, I know that simply is not an option. I have instead decided to make the best of the hand I was dealt and try to help other people see that life does still go on.

500 WORDS THAT DESCRIBE WHAT IT FEELS LIKE TO LOSE YOUR MOTHER

It sucks. It is sad, it is lonely, it is heart breaking, it is life changing, it is painful, it is tragic, it is pathetic, it is devastating, it is depressing…it is just so damn bad. You feel as if your life will never go on. There is a void that can never be filled because there is no other love in this world like the love of a mother. There is so much that she has missed and will miss. It rips you up and tears you down. You feel empty, you feel lost. It leaves a huge gaping hole in your heart that will never, ever heal. It messes with your mind. It brings anger into your heart, anger than you know your mother wouldn't want you to feel, but you feel it anyway. You'll miss her, probably more than you'll ever miss anybody in this entire world. It's a roller-coaster of emotions. One minute you'll be at peace with her death the next you'll feel the heart wrenching feeling that she is never coming back. Hearing her name will pull at you, it will leave you feeling unsettled, especially when you know that she is missing extreme milestones in your life. It is dark, it is upsetting, it is miserable. There's regret, there's guilt, and there is an extreme feeling of loss that could never,

ever be replaced. But when you think of her, as a person rather than a lost loved one, and all of the moments the two of you have shared together, each and every lovely memory will flood through your mind. Think of her before she died, the love she had for you will always outweigh her death. She didn't leave you because she wanted to, she left because there were other plans for her, and she was greater than this world. When you think of your mother, you feel happiness, you feel content, you feel loved, you feel overwhelmed, you feel enamored, you feel comfort, you feel lifted, you feel blessed, you feel honored, you feel inspired, you feel hopeful, you feel strong, you feel brave, you feel encouraged, you feel like you again. And when you finally realize that life continues on, you realize you are here to live it, and live it for her. You remember the kind of life she wanted for you, and that's a happy life. You feel her in the wind and you see her in the stars, she visits you in your dreams and she guards you with all of her heart. But most importantly, when you think of your mother, remember that she is constantly guiding you and sending you love when you need it the most. You will feel refreshed, you will feel her hug, you will feel her heart and that is when you will feel brand new. And each and every day you will realize that you have all of these feelings because you were lucky enough to call her your mother.

LIFE AFTER LOSING A PARENT

"You are now forced to cope with the loss of parental love and attention that was given uniquely to you, and that you depended on, possibly even took for granted."

-Carol Staudacher

Saying goodbye to a parent is one of the hardest things to do in life. It is also something that almost everyone goes through.

Unfortunately, like myself, some go through it earlier than others. Losing a parent is like a loss of childhood. No other bond exists like the one with a mother or father.

After my mom's passing, weeks went by, the weeks turned into months. Day by day everything started to change. These days slowly started to turn into my "new normal."

The summer following Mom's passing, butterflies followed me everywhere. I was given a butterfly bush by a co-worker; we planted it near the house. Along with the butterfly bush was a note. It read "Look for that special butterfly, the one that keeps on coming back." And there was one very pretty one that always returned. I like to think that was my mom popping in to check on us every now and again.

We celebrated my mom's 49th birthday, but this time she wasn't here to celebrate with us. We wrote notes attached to balloons and sent them up to our angel in heaven.

Thanksgiving and Christmas flew by. It was not the same without her, we tried to stick to the traditions, but we all missed her so very much. I had a Christmas ornament made in her memory. It was a beautiful heart with doves and hand written on it was, "All hearts come home for Christmas, Our Beautiful Angel, Gina."

The New Year came, the first New Year ever without her by my side. I remembered the statue that I had given her the year before, "Every day is a gift, each year a new beginning." It was a new beginning, the beginning of a new life for me. And each day is a certainly is gift.

I experienced most of the firsts without my mom. I celebrated my 25th birthday as her one year "Angelversary" quickly approached; I remember looking back and realizing how far I've come after that first year without her, and I now look ahead to see how much further I will go.

IS A HOUSE REALLY A HOME IF YOUR LOVED ONE IS GONE?

Never in a million years did I think I would be standing up in front of hundreds of people at my mother's funeral, reading her eulogy. But I did. And that was my new reality.

The smell of Sunday spaghetti dinners, the movie nights, the family bonding, the holidays, the bon fires, hearing my mom yell "Dinner is ready!", the laughter, the love, Christmas morning. Everything, and I mean EVERYTHING, now seemed so distant.

Before my mom was diagnosed I would say we were an average middle class family with everything we needed. Love being one of them, and man, was there so much love in that house of ours. It was just the four of us – me, my older sister, my mom, and my dad. Happy, healthy, and most importantly, content. Of course we had our ups and downs, just as any family does, but the four of us had a bond that was unbreakable. We were blessed.

Our family went from four to three, overnight. Being in that house without my mom seemed so wrong. After all, she was the one who made that house our home. Each day it seemed as if she would walk through the door at any moment and my whole nightmare would end. But she wasn't going to. She wasn't coming back and I had to accept that.

I often think to myself how could we ever leave this house? After all, my sister and I grew up here. It was the first house my parents ever owned. How could we possibly bag up all of her belongings, throw them in the trash and just leave?

Is a house really a home if your loved one is gone? No. It's not. Because a house, in fact, is just a house. A family is what makes it a home. Just because that house is the only place I've ever known her doesn't change the fact that my mom is no longer physically with us, in our house, and is now in an urn in our living room with "Our Angel, Gina" engraved on it. Memories were just made in that house, but in my mind is where they will always stay. Leaving there would never make me miss or love her any less than I do and the memories I've had with her can never be physically taken away.

And just as I thought the world would never go on after my mother died, somehow it did. As much as I would love to hold on to everything forever, I can't. And it sucks. But just because you move on with your life does not mean you are forced to forget your lost loved ones. They are always tucked away in your broken heart and will stay there forever. And in due time you will figure out a way to live creatively with that bruised and broken heart of yours. Just like I did.

GRIEVING: IT'S A PERSONAL THING

Once you have to actually go through the sorrow of mourning somebody you loved so very much, you'll look back and ask yourself how the hell you've made or are making it through. The first few days or even weeks after losing somebody, you won't understand why they are no longer here. They say people grieve in stages. Denial, Anger, Bargaining, Depression, Acceptance. I don't believe that everybody goes through those exact stages.

Mourning the loss of a loved one, to me, is a very personal thing. There will be a lot of emotions, backtracking, moving forward, and then back tracking again. There will be ups and downs. You may feel like your life is one big roller coaster ride, but that's okay. It just means you are working through it all in your own way, in your own time, on YOUR own terms.

I remember Googling the "stages of grief" so I could prepare myself for what to expect. It has been almost four years since my mom has passed away and I may still be in the denial process, or maybe that's my mind's way of protecting my heart from breaking any more than it already has, but I find different ways to go on.

Just like you, I go through many different emotions but I believe it is a day-by-day process. I go from having a day where I feel at peace, to having a day where I want to curl up in a ball and cry. Some days I feel I have lost my way, but I force myself to get back on track to the healing process. It's all about finding a way to continue on a happy life while still keeping the "lost" memories close to your heart.

It's very hard to know what to say to someone you love who lost somebody so close to their heart. You may be afraid of saying the wrong thing, or making the person feel even worse. While you may never be able to take away the pain of the loss, you can in fact help them by reminding them you remembered the person they lost has lived.

"If you know someone who has lost a loved one, and you're afraid to mention them because you think you might make them sad by reminding them that they died – you're not reminding them. They didn't forget they died. What you're reminding, them of is that you remembered that they lived, and that is a great, great gift."
–Elizabeth Edward

LOSING MY MOTHER, FINDING MYSELF

There truly is no other love in this world like the love of the mother. And man, the love I received from my mother was truly incredible.

She taught me so much, she taught me everything. How to love, how to care, how to feel, how to forgive, and most importantly, how to live.

She was my rock, my heart, my best friend. She was the only person in this world who would ever fully understand me and love me unconditionally.

As my 23rd birthday came and went, I held the world in the palm of my hands. I had everything I could ever want and everything I could ever need right in front of me.

Until that horrible day in July of 2012 when my family and I received the heart wrenching news that the spot they found on my mother's lung was in fact cancer. Stage four lung cancer no less. One of the deadliest and most aggressive forms.

My world stopped.

Everything I had worked for suddenly didn't matter anymore. Everything that seemed so big all of a sudden looked so small. My life was turned upside-down in an instant.

My mother was about to face the biggest fight of her life and I knew how hard she would fight, not for herself, but for her family and all of those who loved her so much.

Knowing somebody you care so deeply about could be ripped from your world in a matter of seconds is a very scary thing. But then again cancer shouldn't make us realize that.

My mom put her brave face on, suited up and was ready for war. But cancer never plays fair and sometimes even the strongest of soldiers don't survive the battle.

My mom became an angel.

The loss of my mother was devastating. I would wake up every morning and wipe my tear soaked eyes, hoping that this would all just be a bad dream. But it wasn't. I didn't exactly know how I would make it through those sad mornings and dark nights, but I did.

Each and every day without her would be one day further apart from her. One more day that she would miss. I was angry. So angry. Not so much for myself, more so for her. I was angry that she would miss so much. Angry that she would never get to see her babies get married, angry that she would never be a grandmother, angry that so much had been ripped away from her.

As time so quickly flew by, I was looking in the mirror unable to recognize the girl staring back at me. I was different now, I was changed for the better. Yes, I lost the most important person in my life, but I gained so much in turn.

I found the things I love, the things I deserve, the things I want, and the things I need. I made it through and became the woman I am today.

Although my mother's physical presence is gone, I hold her in my heart every day.

.

THE THINGS I HOPE MY MOTHER KNEW

Often times when we lose somebody we love so much, we look back and wish we had told them so much more than we actually did. After losing my mother so many thoughts have popped into my mind…so many thoughts I hope she knew.

I hope she knew how hard I fought to save her life. Although she had a terminal illness, I still never gave up on hope. The minute my mom was diagnosed with stage four lung cancer, I researched anything and everything I could that would help her. The last week of her life I tried everything I could to save her, even if it was only for a few more days. Time just wasn't on my side, but I hope she knew I tried with all my might.

I hope she knew that she taught me what unconditional love truly is. The love she had for me and my sister was truly unconditional. She was the kind of person who would do anything for anybody. She taught me the true meaning of the word family. She loved me until her very last breath, but I hope she knew I knew that.

I hope she knew that in my eyes there was nobody in this world above her. My mom was so cool. The "Fun" mom. The life of the party. She brought so much energy wherever she went. She taught me how to dance, she taught me how to be myself, and she taught me how to go out there and get what I want. There are few people in this world that I will ever hold above her, and I hope she knew.

I hope she knew that I was sorry. Sorry for all of the torture I put her through as I went through my teenage years. Sorry for all the bad things I said to her out of anger. Sorry for not being the best daughter I could be. I am sorry mom, and I hope you knew that.

I hope she knew how much laughter she brought into my life. My mother was hilarious. She would say and do the funniest things. I was recently looking back at old Facebook posts of hers and I came across something she had posted "If you think no one cares if you're alive, try missing a few credit card payments." I saw that an instantly started laughing. Where did she come up with this stuff? She still continues to make me laugh even after she is gone, I hope she knew she would.

I hope she knew how much she would be missed. When you are confronted with the horrible news that you have terminal stage four lung cancer, I guess you pretty much prepare for the worst. I think in the back of my mom's mind she knew she wouldn't make it past a year, and she was in fact right. After leaving behind two daughters and a loving husband, along with so many others who loved her. Did she know how much I would miss her? I hope she knew.

I hope she knew that because of her I would never settle for less than I deserve. My mom was a go-getter. She took everything she wanted with a smile. She was always kind to others but did not put up with anybody's shit. Because of her

I will never again settle in any type of relationship, whether it be a friendship or a romantic relationship. She opened up my eyes to all that I deserve. I hope she knew.

I hope she knew that she would continue to inspire long after she's gone. During her entire battle with cancer, my mom remained so positive. She would post an inspirational saying each and every morning on Facebook. The amount of love, support, and prayers she received was endless. She inspired so many, and I will never stop sharing her story. She made a mark on this world, I hope she knew that she would.

I hope she knew that all I would become after she passed away, is owed to her. After the heart break of my mom's passing, so much good entered my life. I found my passion in writing. I'd like to think all of the blessings that have come my way over the years that she has been gone were sent from heaven, from her. I took everything bad and turned it into something amazing, I hope she knew I would.

I hope she knew that although I would miss her tremendously, I would be okay. My mom was a worry wart. Constantly checking up on me to see where I was, what I was doing, if I had my seat belt on, if I needed food, etc. I guess that's just what moms do. I truly hope she knew that because of all she has taught me, I would be okay after her passing. I hope she knew that I would go on and try to live the happiest life I could. It's all because of her that I am okay, I hope she knew that.

I hope she heard me tell her I love her just seconds before she took her last breath. May 27th, 2013 at 11:53 pm. It was the day I was called back to the hospital because my mom's heart rate was sky high. I knew she was sick, but never in a million years did I think that would be the last time I would see her, hold her hand, or tell her I love her ever again. Seconds before my mom's heart gave up, I grabbed her ice cold hand, in the panic filled medical ICU room, and told her I loved her. I hope she heard me.

I hope she knew that it was her that made me fully understand the meaning of the word "HOPE". I will never, ever forget that day, July 19th, 2012. The day my mother sat me down and the words poured out of her mouth… "Jenna, I have stage four lung cancer that has spread to my lymph nodes and bones, but I will be OKAY. I promise you that I will never give up, I have so much HOPE." She said. She held onto that very same hope throughout her entire battle and I hope she knew she taught me what HOPE truly is.

I hope she still knows how much I love her.

TO THE MOTHERLESS ON
MOTHER'S DAY

Today sucks, I know. It's going to be hard. But so is every other day since you have lost your mother. There is absolutely no love in this world like the love of a mother. There is a void that cannot and will not ever be filled, no matter what anybody tells you. You don't miss her today any more than you will tomorrow, or the next day, or the day after that. Today, Mother's Day, is just another painful reminder that she is no longer physically here. As you watch friends celebrate with their moms, please remember that yours is tucked away deep down in your heart where she will forever stay. As the wind blows through your hair, know that it is her gentle and loving touch. As the warmth of the sun shines on your face please remember the warmth in your mother's heart through all of the days she had on this earth. She didn't want to ever leave you and she still hasn't left you. Your mother was greater than this world. I know sometimes life just doesn't seem fair and it never will, but please, please don't cry today for your mother would want nothing more than to see you smile. I feel the pain within your heart as another day passes by without her. She doesn't want you to be sad. She wants you to honor her life in the best way possible and that way is to live it. Live it for you. Live it for her.

I have come to find that the best way to heal is to remember. Remember her. Remember the sorrow, remember the love, remember everything. Talk to her, she's always listening. And simply cherish the time you did have with her and the memories you have made. I want you to know that on this day, you are not alone. You are never alone. All of our mothers are watching over us from heaven this Mother's Day… and every day, for the rest of our lives.

Happy Mother's Day to all of the motherless out there. Today is your day too. Celebrate her, start a new tradition, live life to the fullest, and most importantly remember that even through the darkest of days, life still goes on.

A LETTER TO HEAVEN ON MOTHER'S DAY

Mom,

I think back to a few years ago when Mother's Day for us was always so simple. We would hangout outside, barbecue, drink, and share a few laughs. You always insisted on cooking although it was supposed to be your day. I can still hear your voice saying "don't get me anything, save your money." You were always so silly like that.

2012 was the last Mother's Day that you were healthy, happy, and cancer free – or so we thought. Fast-forward one year to 2013, I knew when I left you that night after spending Mother's Day with you, that my life would never, ever be the same. You were so beautiful yet you were so sick. Stage four lung cancer was stealing you away from so many people who loved you so very much – yet you still fought with everything you had in you. Until 15 short days later when my life was turned upside down and you were taken away from this world way too soon. 48 years old. Never in my wildest nightmares would I imagine becoming a motherless daughter at the age of 24. Never in my wildest nightmares did I think I would be celebrating a Mother's Day without you. And never in my wildest nightmares did I think this would happen to us.

As I approach every Mother's Day here without you I cannot help but wonder why bad things happen to good people? Why did you have to die? Why are you not here? Why do I have to go through this day and every other Mother's Day without you, for the rest of my life?

Well the truth is I don't, and the truth is I won't. Because although I can no longer physically see you, or hold your hand, or hear your laugh, I can feel you around me every single day. You guide me and lead me to the places I have gone and to the places I have yet to go.

Although you left this world long before you should have I know and feel it in my heart that you still continue to love me, to teach me, and to send me your strength. So on this Mother's Day, Mom, I will not cry because I miss you beyond words, I will smile because I had the best 24 years of my life with you. I will smile

*because I knew you, and I will smile because I love you
with all my heart and soul and the bond we had could
never, ever be broken.*

Happy Mother's Day in Heaven, Mom.

I miss you.

THE THINGS WE MUST LET GO OF IN ORDER TO MOVE FORWARD

Losing someone who you love and care about so very deeply is one of the hardest things on this earth to go through. I remember throughout my teen years, never having experienced a loss before, I would think to myself, what will I do when my grandma dies? How will I ever live without her? After all she was the oldest one in our family. My natural instinct was to think that she would be the first to leave this world. Some nights I would cry myself to sleep over it. All of those thoughts would run through my mind and I would try to snap myself out of it, telling myself to stop worrying so much.

As a writer, my main goal is to help others along on their grief journey. I want to open up their hearts and let a new light shine in to make others see that if I could go on without the most important person in my life, they can too.

I compiled a list of things that I let go of shortly after my mother died, and I am certain that those are the things that are helping me heal. Although everyone grieves at their own pace and in their own way, I do believe that we can all make it out to the other side, step by step, day by day, and live a happy life again.

Anger & Hate. You may feel angry at yourself, angry at a doctor who couldn't save your loved ones life, angry at the world. I always say that anger and hate are heavy bags to carry and we must let them go. We must put those bags down in order to let new love into our hearts. This doesn't mean we are forgetting our loved ones or pushing their death to the side. It simply means we are finding a way to move forward, finding a way to learn how to love again, and finding a way to live with a bruised and broken heart.

Negativity. After my mom died I decided I would rid myself of any negativity lingering in my life. This meant making amends with people whom I never thought I could, changing the places I go, changing my way of thinking, and even getting rid of some "friends." I decided to no longer let the small things get to me. In order to heal we must make peace in all aspects of our lives.

Jealousy. Sometimes I feel a bit jealous when I see people who have survived cancer longer than my mother. It's not that I would ever want anything to happen to these people, I just feel as if my mother and our family were cheated out of so much. Cancer took everything from me. I used to see girls my age out shopping with their mother's and I would get so frustrated and upset. When put in that situation I have trained myself to remember memories of shopping with my own mother rather than getting jealous or upset. It has made a world of a difference.

The feeling of abandonment. I always ask myself, is it better for someone to leave you by death or by choice? And I have come to the conclusion that it is better to be left by death. My mother didn't want to leave me, she didn't want to leave any of us. I know in my heart of hearts that she fought for as long as she could, not for herself, but for her family.

Shutting out the world. Picking up writing was one of the best things I could have ever done after losing my mom. I didn't want to be one of those people who shuts out the world and I started to feel like that was what I was doing. Sharing her story through my previous book, Life Goes On..?, has helped me tremendously. If you need to talk to someone, go to a friend. If you need to vent, vent. If you want to cry, cry. If you want to share your story, share it. It will help.

Living in the past. Of course we always want to remember our lost loved ones, and we should. But we cannot sit around and wonder what could have been or what should have been. Bringing our loved ones back is just not an option. So instead we must make goals for the future, live our lives to the fullest and remember that our lost loved ones would want us to lead a happy life and leading a happy life is one of the best ways to honor them.

WHAT IT'S LIKE TO DATE A GIRL WITHOUT A MOTHER

She'll be a different kind of girl. She has experienced loss and knows what it feels like to be left, even if it was unintentionally. Every day her heart will be hurting, even if she doesn't show it. Comfort her.

She will act tough, she will pretend she doesn't have emotions. She does. They're tucked away deep down inside her broken heart. Let her know she is meant to be loved and you want to love her.

Each and every time you mention your mother she will cringed, not at the thought of her, but at the thought of her own mother not being around anymore. She will feel a sense of embarrassment when someone asks her about her parents. It is one of the hardest things in the world to have to explain to somebody why and how you are a motherless daughter.

Holidays will always be hard for her, after all the most important person in her world is no longer there. Do something to honor and celebrate her mother.

She will wish with all of her might that you got to meet her mother before she died, but she knows that is not a possibility. She constantly wonders if her mother would like you, would she approve of you? Get to know her mother through her. Ask questions. Don't be afraid of bringing up what you think may harm her heart even more. It won't. She loves to talk about her mother. She wants you to know every little detail, but she probably would never tell you that on her own. Talk to her, ask her what her mother was like, what her mother loved to do, what her favorite food was, what song she liked, what she learned from her, etc. These questions will open her up to you, even if it's only a tiny bit. Remind her every day that she is beautiful and she was raised by a queen.

She will cry a lot but you won't know it when she does. Let her know it is okay and let her know that you want to be the shoulder she cries on. Let her know you want to be the one to make her smile through all the tears.

She'll want to take a lot of pictures. Memories are gold to her. She knows what it's like to have amazing memories ripped from under her feet, and she is more than thankful for the pictures she has taken to keep those memories alive.

She will hide, she will not accept your love right away and it will take her a while to realize she is more than deserving of it. She will hate the fact that she feels this way, remember she can't help it.

She will be very independent, there will be a lot of things she won't need you for, be there for her anyway, but always give her space. She values her solitude but don't ever be offended by it. Take the time to understand why she likes to be alone.

She is not broken, although it may seem she is, so please don't try to fix her. She is just finding her way in this world without her mother's guidance. She will guard her heart more than she ever has before, and you'll have to try very hard to climb her walls, but when you eventually get to the other side, it will all be worth it, because she will love you with everything she has left in her.

THINGS TO KNOW BEFORE DATING A "MOTHERLESS" GIRL

She will appreciate your patience. She may unexpectedly get upset every now and then, she may even take her frustrations out on you. Be patient with her, she just wants you to understand the magnitude of her loss.

Your trust must be earned. She knows what it feels like to be left, she knows what it feels like to be let down- even if it was unintentionally. She will have her doubts about you and she will have the fear of you leaving but earning her trust is the key to everything.

Pictures mean the world. They say if you want to know what someone is afraid of losing, pay close attention to what they photograph. She knows how precious life is and she knows just how short it can be. She will want to cherish all of her favorite memories with her. Smile for the camera and let her know that you want the same.

Her alone time is valuable. Plain and simple,

sometimes she may just want to be alone. Realize that it has nothing to do with you and everything to do with her.

Loss can bring out insecurities, ones she never even knew she had. At some points she may not feel pretty enough, smart enough, nice enough, etc. There will be times she will question why you love her. Love her anyway and make sure you show her every day.

Don't pity her and don't show her you feel sorry for her. Instead, take the time to understand her past, to understand her future goals. Most importantly, take the time to truly understand her. It is not her fault that she lost her mother, it is not her fault when she thinks thoughts she can't help thinking. There will be times she will cry out of nowhere. Be there for her.

She doesn't need you, she wants you. When a girl loses her mother, she loses her world. You must understand that if a girl can make it through that tremendous loss, she can make it through any loss. If you are in her life it will never be because she needs you in it, it will be because she wants you in it. Realize just how lucky you are to have someone special like her.

MY MOTHER'S EULOGY

This was one of the hardest things I have ever had to do besides leaving the hospital the night cancer stole her from my world. As I spoke the words below almost four years ago, I can still feel the pound of my heart and hear the sadness in my own voice. I remember clearly as I read those words from my crumbled up piece of notebook paper- I looked around and I saw so many tears but I also saw so many smiling faces.

Tears from all of us who will miss her so very much and smiling faces from all who got a chance to know her. I left the funeral home that day with the comfort of knowing how loved she was, how inspiring she was, and how many lives she has touched in her short time here.

June 1ˢᵗ, 2013
My mother's celebration of life memorial.

"24 years ago I laid eyes on one of the best people to ever step foot on this earth. I can't put into words the love she had for her family and friends. She brought joy to

many, whether it was for a minute or for a lifetime. She was and always will be an inspiration to so many people. Despite the fact that she had a terminal cancer, she still always put others first. When she was first diagnosed, she did not look at it as a death sentence. She looked at it as more of a reason to go out there and live the life she loved. She never judged anyone; she always saw the good in every person she met. She was the perfect wife to my Dad, a loving mother to me and my sister, an amazing cousin, and a supportive friend. She will one day be an amazing grandma from heaven. She was a simple person with a simple life; she never asked for much, all she wanted was more time with the people she loved so deeply. She taught me to always be kind to others and to treat people exactly the way I want to be treated, and that I will carry with me forever. She is free of pain now & has flown away with the angels. Mom, we will be counting down the days until we get to see you again, I love you."

THE ANSWERS I WISH I HAD

What kind of wedding would she imagine for me?

Since the most important person will not be physically there to witness me someday get married, I look back now and wish I had talked to my mom more about ideas for when the day finally does come. I would love to know her opinion on wedding songs, father-daughter dance, color themes, places, and photography.

Kids Names.

One thing I know my mom always wanted was to one day be a grandmother. Unfortunately she won't even be a grandma here on earth but one thing I will make sure of, when the time comes, is that my kids will know all about her, the kind of person she was and how much she loved them even though she never met them. I wish I had asked her what names she likes, if she thought I would have a boy or a girl first. Simple stuff like that, that I wish I could ask her now.

How she put up with all my crap over the

years.

I was no angel growing up, I was a little (actually a lot) hard to handle. From sneaking out and drinking at age 14 to skipping class constantly, I look back and realize how much torture I put my parents through. Karma is going to bite me in the ass when I do have children and I wish more than anything, when that day comes, that my mom would be here to give me advice on handling a wild child like myself.

Her homemade spaghetti and meatballs recipe.

Sunday dinner was rarely ever missed at my house. My mom would make sure that Sunday would be the one day we are all together for dinner. She would start cooking her homemade sauce and her perfect meatballs early every Sunday morning and man, do I miss that meal.

Where is her wedding dress?

I would love to see it and try it on. Although she was a little shorter than I am she was about the same size as me when she got married 29 years ago.

What is the craziest thing she has ever done?

My mom, like me, was a wild child also. She was the fun mom, the "cool" mom. She knew how to party and she didn't put up with any body's shit. I would love to know the craziest thing she has ever done.

What kind of man she thought I would wind up with?

My mom had always loved my boyfriends, she would immediately make them part of the family. I knew she loved the guy I was dating when she was sick, but I knew she knew he wasn't the one. I've dated guys after I left him and the first thought on my mind is "what would mom think of him?

Was she scared to die?

I know that she didn't want to leave her loved ones behind, but she was in so much pain towards the end. She had always put on a brave face and I rarely saw her shed a tear, but I want to know if she knew she was dying, was she scared? Did she believe that she will be able to watch over us? Did she know I was there every second on her final days? Did she know I tried everything I could to save her life? Did she know how much I truly loved her?

SEVEN REASONS WHY THERE IS NOONE IN THIS WORLD LIKE YOUR MOTHER

Because her love for you will always be unconditional. I am not a mother, but my own mother sure did a wonderful job of expressing her unconditional love for me and my sister. Though she is no longer physically with me, I can lay my head down to sleep each night knowing that she will never stop loving me.

Because she will ALWAYS have your back. No matter what you do, no matter how many rules you break, no matter how many times you get a speeding ticket, no matter what- who will always have your back? Your mother.

Because she gave you life. Child labor is painful. Your mother carried you for nine months and endured the pain of labor, all for you.

Because she will always forgive you. You can be in a bad mood, you can basically tell her off, make her cry but no matter what she will always forgive you and take you back into her loving arms.

Because she has made many sacrifices for you. She has sacrificed her life to make yours better.

Because she is the glue that keeps your family together.

Because she is your safe haven. A sad, lonely, heartbroken you walks into the arms of your mother and nothing can seem anymore uplifting. All of your stress will wash away and you are at peace in her arms.

DEAR CANCER, I HATE YOU

Dear Cancer,

I hate you. You suck. You're terrible. You are the true definition of a heart breaker. You single handedly ruined my entire life in the matter of ten short months. You took away my best friend, the only person in this world who will ever love me unconditionally, my mother. And you took her in the most horrible way possible. You stopped her heart from beating at the young age of 48. You crushed my future and tore my family apart. You broke all of our hearts, so many of us. You stole my mother's dreams of seeing her baby girls get married, or becoming a grandmother, or spending the rest of her life with the love of her life, my father. You forced me to witness things no person should ever have to witness and you've forced my mother to endure pain that goes beyond the physical aspects. Not only have you taken away my mother but you've taken away so many other important people. The same thing that drives me to live after this loss is the same reason I hate you, cancer. But cancer, you did not win the day my mother gained her angel wings. You did not beat her. She beat you, as she left this world with her love, her hope, her strength, her bravery, and her dignity, surrounded by the people who she loved the most. You may have destroyed a lot but you have in turn taught me lessons I never thought I would learn by age 27. You showed me just how short and precious life truly is. You showed me that everyday truly is a gift and that I should never take anything or anybody for granted. You have forced me to recognize a strength within myself that I never knew I had. Cancer, although I hate you with all of my heart, you have brought out the woman in me that my mother always hoped I would be. I will never forgive you for taking away the best person I'll ever know and I will never let you take away what made her that woman. You may have taken her life but you will never, ever take away the way she lived it and the love she shared. Cancer that is why you did not win.

WOMAN ON HOSPICE DECRIBES WHAT DYING FEELS LIKE

As a grief/inspiration blogger I receive several messages per day. All which are emotional as I hear stories of life, stories of hope, and stories of heartache from people around the world. About a year ago I received a message from a special lady who reached out to me telling me she needed inspiration. The more I talked to her the more she reminded me of my beautiful mother.

I often think people are put into our lives at certain times, for certain reasons. To teach us lessons, to help us heal, to inspire us, to open our eyes to so much more; and even to break our hearts open so new love is welcomed in. These kind of people are the special kind that you wish you could hold onto forever. The ones who don't deserve the pain and suffering but for some reason they have to go through it.

Life just is not fair sometimes and I can't

seem to make sense of it all.

The most heartbreaking thing about a mother who is fighting cancer is knowing that she will have to leave her children behind. I can't help but cry every time I think about what my mother thought knowing she had to leave me and my sister. Knowing that she would never be here to see us buy a house, or get married, or have children, or all the things mothers are supposed to be there for. It breaks my heart and after talking to this amazing woman I felt compelled to share her story which so many people can relate to.

"My name Lynn. Here I am, 34 years old, and I am in the end stages of ovarian cancer. I am staring death right in the face. It shouldn't be much longer until I go. I am on hospice as we speak. The cancer has spread to my bones and it hurts terribly. I cry. I beg God to let me die because I can no longer take this pain. The hardest part of dying is knowing I will be leaving my children. My son who is eight and my daughter who is six.

What am I thinking? I am thinking about friends,

and places, and dogs that I've had. I am thinking about how I love Billy Joel and the Beatles. My favorite song in the world is "Imagine." I love to write and I love to paint. I cannot eat anymore but I was addicted to sour patch kids for a few years. I so badly wish I could have some right now. I love my children and I love my pain medication. I am thinking about what will happen after I die and where I will go. I am thinking about death and I am feeling so angry that soon there will be no more me. I am thinking about my little girl with soft eyes and an attitude towards life that makes me feel so small. I have written hundreds of letters to my kids – for every upcoming birthday, for their graduations, and for their weddings.

I am so blessed to have lived 34 years and to have two beautiful children. I am blessed that I get the chance to say goodbye to them and I believe that everything terrible that we go through prepares us for the journey ahead.

In a way, I think dying is beautiful. I know I have very little time left and it really puts life into perspective." -Lynn

To Lynn, an amazing person I've met along my own healing journey. May the road ahead be as peaceful as possible for you and your beautiful children and when the time comes I know the angels will lead you in.

*Lynn passed away only five short days after sending this to me.

I ASKED 15 PEOPLE IF THEY THINK HEAVEN IS A REAL PLACE, THIS IS WHAT THEY SAID

"Heaven is under our feet as well as over our heads."

"I believe Heaven is real. I believe the soul has to go somewhere and watch over their loved ones. I also believe that everyone has their own Heaven with the people that they want there. It is not necessarily what everyone depicts it as with pearly gates and such."

"I'd like to think so... I'd like to think that there is a place you go after you die that you just don't cease to exist."

"I believe Heaven is a real place. Besides being taught that in the Bible, I believe this because I have too much to lose if I don't. I think Heaven is not only a place but a feeling of hope and if I don't have hope, what's the point? I want to be reunited with my loved ones who have passed and Heaven gives me the hope that I will be. What kind of life would this be if we were all put here just to die and vanish into thin air? There has to be something bigger, something greater worth living for after we pass. Somewhere that makes all the pain and suffering we experience in this life worth living through. So yes, I full heartily believe that there is a Heaven and one day we will all be there, reunited with our loved ones, with no more pain, suffering, illnesses, etc. In this place we will finally be made whole and that's where our real fairy-tale will begin!"

"I recently lost my father in law to cancer and if I didn't believe in heaven before I most certainly do now."

"I think heaven is a real place to those who need something to believe in when something horrific happens. Such as a family member passing or when a loved one is sick. It is only natural for us to hope there is a happy/beautiful place where we can all meet again when we die. Heaven makes the grieving process easier. However, the reality of heaven…it is hard to fathom. This world can be very dirty and cruel, I think the idea of Heaven is what people use to make it through life. At this point in my life, no, I do not think Heaven is a real place."

"I do believe we do go somewhere and I am not sure where, but our souls definitely go somewhere."

"I definitely feel that Heaven can be a real thing. I've always have that feeling that family members who have moved on from this life are in a place where there is no wrong doing and everyone is back to being healthy. I always think that one day I will be able to see all the members of my family and also close friends again."

"Great question. Unfortunately my answer is in the middle. I don't know if Heaven exits because fortunately I am alive."

"I believe heaven is real. We have to be naive

to think we are the only life form in the whole universe. Maybe Heaven is like another planet where you can be whoever you want, whatever you want. You live there forever where you never age, or get sick, or feel pain."

"I think that there is some type of afterlife where you get to be reunited with your loved ones."

"I believe Heaven is the Universe. When spirits/souls enter into Heaven they are given a gift, the universe. They can go anywhere, anytime, and have beautiful and magical experiences. All their Earth experiences that were not good will be removed and the spirits/souls will only feel the love they felt and gave on earth."

"I'm not really sure. I'd like to think that Heaven is real but I have a hard time understanding it all."

"I believe in Heaven. It's nice to think there is something amazing after the life you live. The way I look at it is atheism is stupid because you have nothing to gain from it and everything to lose. What's it going to hurt if you believe and you are wrong? But if you don't believe in heaven and you are wrong then what? So for me, I'd rather believe and like to think there's another life out there for me."

"Yes, Heaven is a real place. I know this."

1,305 DAYS SINCE CANCER TOOK YOU AWAY

1,305 days since I last saw your beautiful face. 1,305 heart breaking days since I last heard your voice, or felt your hug, or witnessed the warmth of your smile. 1,305 days since you last told me you loved me as I watched you take your very last breathe. 1,305 days too many without you here on earth. 1,305 days since I held your hand, or felt your touch, or watched you look at me proudly. 1,305 days since my entire world was turned upside down as I watched you slip away. 1,305 days since you spoke your wise words of wisdom, or helped someone in need. 1,305 days since I fought as hard as I could to save your life. 1,305 days since I swore you'd hold on for one more day. 1,305 days that felt like eternity but flew by too fast. 1,305 days that you have been ignorant of all that has happened. 1,305 days with you on my mind every single waking moment. 1,305 nights full of wonderful dreams of you, only to wake up and realize it is the day times without you that are a nightmare.

1,305 days..

1,305 damn days..

Without you.

But none of those 1,305 days could ever outweigh the 8,834 best days of my life were spent with you in it. I miss you.

THE THINGS MY MOTHER'S BATTLE WITH CANCER TAUGHT ME

It taught me that life just isn't fair and life is just too damn short.

My mother's battle with cancer taught me what courage truly is. I watched my mom suffer through a lot of physical and emotional pain, more pain than a soul should ever have to see and never once did I hear her complain. She was so strong and so brave. When I had to read her eulogy in front of hundreds who came to pay their respects, in that moment I realized my own strength, strength I never knew I had. Strength that I knew came from her.

It taught me that love never dies, even after a person does. My relationship with my mother did not end the day she died. It continues every single day. I truly believe that she still teaches me lessons. She loved me and my sister more than anything in the world and I can still feel her love although she is no longer physically here.

It taught me how beautiful life is. As I watched my mom battle cancer my heart broke. I remember all of the beauty that remained as I was so extremely lucky to have had her in my life for the 24 years that I did. We made so many beautiful memories together, ones that I will never forget. Sometimes we have to experience sadness to understand what happiness truly is.

It taught me that nothing lasts forever. Not the good or the bad. All things eventually do pass. The pain and sorrow in my heart in time will fade away and although I miss my mother every second of my life, I find comfort in believing that I will one day be with her again.

HIDDEN TREASURES LEFT BEHIND

Two days after my mom passed away, my family and I were preparing the picture-board posters for her Celebration of Life Memorial. My father was upstairs looking for more photos when he ran down the stairs and told us he had found a letter my mom had left behind for us. It was tucked away in her jewelry box. My mom was not the best speller/writer in the world but this letter melted my heart.

The letter read:

"To Bob, Kristina & Jenna-

When you see butterflies and lady bugs it will be me watching over you all. Tell your kids how much I love them even before they were born. Dad will make a great grandpa. I will watch over my family. I love you all!"

After finding that first letter we found several others she left behind that told the story of her undying love for our family.

CREATIVE THINGS TO DO WITH YOUR MOMS ASHES

Memorial jewelry. Before my mom passed away she insisted that when she dies, me, my sister, my grandma, and her closest cousins all get a necklace made with her ashes in it. We got them at the funeral home while planning her services. It is a great way to keep them close to your heart...literally.

Spread them in the place she loved the most. This obviously isn't the most creative idea, but what is better than bringing her ashes to her favorite place in the entire world and sprinkling them there. A piece of her will always be in the place she loved.

Get a tattoo. Now a days you can get a tattoo with your loved ones ashes in the ink. Sounds crazy but it can be done.

Fireworks. Watch your angel take flight by putting some of their ashes into fireworks.

Balloons. Put ashes into a helium balloon by using a funnel cup and then blow the balloon up and watch it soar. You can even send a message to heaven by writing on the balloon with a marker.

In a painting. Just simply add her ashes to paint. Whether it be wall paint, a hand panting, whatever you'd like.

THE BATTLE YOU DIDN'T CHOOSE

"Choose your battles wisely. After all, life isn't measured by how many times you stood up to fight. It's not winning battles that makes you happy, but it's how many times you turned away and chose to look into a better direction. Life is too short to spend it on warring. Fight only the most, most, most important ones, let the rest go."
— *C. JoyBell C.*

Mom,

"Every day you have a choice, life is all about the choices you make." Words that I can still hear you say, as if it were just yesterday, even after a year and a half without you physically here. I can't even recall how many times you have told me that. Truer words have never been spoken. Life is all about choices and ultimately the choices people make each and every day will determine their future.

"Battles. Pick and choose yours wisely." Words you would tell me whenever I got frustrated, upset, or angry at something or someone. You, mom, always picked your battles wisely. You knew what was worth the upset and what simply was not.

But on July 19th, 2012 you were faced with a battle that you did not choose. A battle that would change all of our lives forever. A battle you didn't ever want to have to fight. But you did. So courageously. "You have cancer." Is something nobody ever wants to hear, especially when it's one of the most deadly forms of cancer.

Although you didn't pick this battle, you still fought with all that you had in you. You were so brave, so strong, and such a fighter. You looked fear in the face and went in like a soldier, like the warrior that you are, the warrior you had always been.

And only ten months after you were forced into this horrible battle, we were forced to say goodbye to you long before we should have ever had to. I can't think of a person more determined than you, with such a love for others, and a great will to live. But cancer does not play fair and cancer does not let you choose whether you live or die. You did not lose that battle. Cancer may have robbed of us of your physical presence but it will never take away the memories you've made and the lives you've touched.

Nobody in this entire world will ever be able to fill the shoes that you left behind. Cancer did not win that day. You won, because you left this world with so much love, so much inspiration, so much hope, and most importantly you left this world just as strong as you were when you came into it.

You left your mark on so many people and you've impacted so many lives, so many more than I think you'd ever know. And because of the choices you have made throughout your 48 years on this earth, you lived a life worth talking about, a story worth telling.

To the battle that you didn't choose but fought anyway. To the fight you had left in you until you took your very last breath. To the most amazing person I will ever know, fly high my angel. I'll be counting down the days until I get to hug you again. I love you with all of my heart.

MOM, ALL I WANT FOR CHRISTMAS IS..

For you to come home. For you to be here with us, where you belong.

Mom, I miss you terribly. I can't begin to express the sadness I feel each and every time I remember that you are never coming back. It hits hard during the holidays, when that seat you belong in at the dinner table is empty. When I don't get that morning "Merry Christmas!" from you. I never did imagine a Christmas without you and I dancing around to Old Italian Christmas songs, but I now face that harsh, harsh reality. That reality is that you are gone, that reality is that you left this world way too soon, at only 48 years old. You should be here. Why aren't you here? When I hear your favorite Christmas song, "Through the years we all will be together, if the fates allow…." I ask myself, why didn't the fates allow? What did you do to deserve to miss out on so much? When I see girls my age Christmas shopping with their mom it is a painful reality that I will never get to do that again.

When I look under the tree I can't help but wonder what gifts you would of gotten this year, what gifts you would have gotten me....screw the gifts, they never mattered to you anyway. All that mattered to you was being alive and well to share another Christmas with your family and friends.

Memories of passed Christmas' flood through my mind and I can't help but remember how great you made Christmas at our house. Come to think of it, you are my Christmas and when I think about what I truly want for Christmas this year, all I can think of is you.

GRIEVING THROUGH THE HOLIDAYS

The holidays are hard, especially when the person we love most is no longer physically here. Here are some things you can do to ease the pain this holiday season.

Start a new tradition. I made a promise to myself that each year I will buy a new ornament in memory of her. It will be like I never spend a Christmas without her.

Don't avoid or cancel the holiday. Although it is so hard and different without our lost loved ones here we must remember that they would still want us to continue on a happy life, not only around Christmas time but all the time.

Have a good cry, let it all out. If you feel like crying, cry. If you feel like screaming, scream. Let it out. Don't hold the pain and sadness in, talk to a friend about it.

Make a difference. Volunteering or helping people who are struggling will often result in you feeling better about yourself. Spend some time at a local soup kitchen, donate a toy to a toy drive, or even send an old friend a Christmas card or a small gift, I promise you it will make you feel better.

In place of buying your lost loved one a gift, buy something for yourself. Shopping has a magical way of lifting our spirits. This holiday season consider buying something for yourself.

Start a holiday journal. I love writing and sharing my thoughts with people. Consider starting a journal and each Christmas write down what you did, how you made it through and one memory of your loved one. Each year you can look back and see how far you have come.

Remember that you are not alone in your grief. Although you may feel no one is hurting as bad as you are, there are so many other people who share the same pain. Join a holiday grief support group or even ask a friend to chat.

Know that life goes on. We must remember that even though we would sometimes like life to stop, it will never stop for anybody or anything. Continue on your life and honor of your loved one not only this holiday season, but every day of your life.

LIFE LESSONS I'VE LEARNED AFTER LOSING MY MOTHER

Through the heart break, change, and devastation I have learned some key points that will help me along with several others on the healing journey.

Nothing lasts forever. Every time it rains, it stops raining. Every time you hurt, you heal. After darkness always comes light and you get reminded of this each and every morning. Bad times make good times better. Nothing lasts forever. Not the good or the bad so we all might as well smile while we are still here.

Love is stronger than death. My relationship with my mom continues on each and every day and will for the rest of my life. I see pieces of her in myself every time I look in the mirror. She lives on through me. When I hear mine and my mom's song "Some Kind of Wonderful" by Grand Funk Railroad I feel as if we are together. Physical planes cannot separate love and I know this to be true.

It will forever be a part of who I am. I've met many people after losing my mom. It's almost as if I want to introduce myself as "Hi, I'm Jenna, I'm 27 years old, I'm a motherless daughter and I lost my mom to lung cancer." The question "So tell me about your parents?" is like nails on a chalk board. Those who truly know me and knew my mom know pretty much every heart breaking detail of the pain I've endured after losing her, but for those who I've recently met or have yet to meet have no idea. Losing my mom has reshaped who I am, how I see the world, and has changed my life forever.

Memories are the greatest. Oh the memories, they flood through my mind all the time. The good memories are more so from before she was diagnosed with cancer. But I will literally NEVER forget the last few days of her life. We shared laughs, cries, and all different types of emotions but the memory I will be forever grateful for occurred just minutes before she died. I knew something was wrong, she was rushed to the Medical ICU where her heart rate was sky high and her blood pressure was dangerously low. My heart was beating out of my chest, I grabbed her hand looked her right in the eyes and my last words to her were "I love you so much". She looked at me, squeezed my hand and she didn't have to say a word, I knew how much she loved me. In that moment I realized that I have received more love from her in my 24 years with her than most receive in a life time.

Some things will just always be out my control. Watching someone you love suffer is one of the worst experiences you can imagine. All you can do is stick by their side, hold their hand, and try to make them smile through the pain. It's a huge sense of helplessness and you want to take on the pain for them but some things will forever be out of your control. I fought endlessly to try to save my mom's life and I just couldn't, there was nothing more I could do but let her know how loved she was.

Music heals. I personally love music, I love songs with deep meanings. One song that makes me smile when I am feeling down is "Footprints in the Sand" by Leona Lewis. Whenever I hear it, it reminds me that my mom will be right next to me for the rest of my life, not physically but I know her spirit will continue to follow me.

Life is for the living so live it. After a tremendous loss I've heard of many people losing themselves or getting caught up in the bad rather than the good. I often find myself doing certain things and I think how unfair it is that my mom isn't here to enjoy the little pleasure that life brings. I also look at it as more a reason to go out and live. I do the things she loved to do, I do the things I love to do, more so now than ever. Life is just too damn short.

To the world you may be one person, but to one person you may be the world. After my mom passed away I felt a strong urge to share her story with anyone who would listen. I even went as far as writing and publishing a book. I figured if I could make it through the worst time of my life than I could help others do the same. I've had random messages online from people telling me how inspiring my mother's story is, I've had strangers come up to me and tell me I've helped them through a loss and this is the most rewarding of it all. Through my book I hope to continue to inspire many more.

"Music has healing power. It has the ability to take people out of themselves for a few hours."

– Elton John

MARC, THE HOSPITAL NURSE

April and May of 2013, I spent the entire month running around, back and forth to and from Morristown Memorial Hospital. She was in the Simon 5 cancer unit. I was drained. I was sad. I was so tired. I was heartbroken. Subconsciously I knew what was coming. I had a big battle ahead of me and that battle was watching my mother fight her own battle with cancer.

The last month of her life took a toll on our entire family, but mostly on her. I remember stopping somewhere to get food and the lady was so rude and mean to me. I literally got in my car and started crying because she just added sadness to everything that was already going on. I thought to myself, "Wow, if she only knew what I was going through, maybe, just maybe she wouldn't have been so heartless." But I am also more than thankful for this special nurse that helped us out probably more than he will ever know. His name was Marc. He walked into my mom's hospital room every couple of hours to check on her and when he walked in the room it was almost as if you could feel the true warmth of his heart. He was so kind, so compassionate, and so positive every single day.

If he was in a bad mood or having a bad day we sure as heck didn't know about it. He did what he could to make us laugh and smile. I hated leaving the hospital because it made me so nervous. What if they forget to check my mom's vitals? What if she needs help but can't find the strength to get a nurse? What if one of the nurses are mean to her and she can't use her voice to speak up? What if she needs something that she can't get to? It may sound crazy but those were the thoughts that ran through my mind each and every time I had to leave there but when Marc was working I felt so at ease. He was just a kind beautiful soul and although he may think it went unnoticed, I will never, ever forget him and what he did for my mother and our family.

Thank you, Marc. You kindness will forever be remembered.

31 THINGS MY MOTHER TAUGHT ME

1. To always be kind to others.
2. But to never take shit from anybody.
3. Never, ever, ever drink and drive.
4. Always dance like nobody is watching.
5. To love with all of my heart.
6. To never bully/make fun of others.
7. That people will always have something negative to say, ignore it.
8. To love the song "Some Kind of Wonderful."
9. To remain positive in all situations.
10. To pick and choice my battles.
11. Not to wear dark lip liner.
12. That everything in life is based on choices.
13. To never settle for less than I deserve.
14. That life is so much more than the materialistic things.
15. That love always comes before money.
16. That trust is the key to a great relationship.
17. How to make a house a home.

18. How to be grateful for life's little blessings.
19. That it doesn't matter where a person came from, everybody bleeds the same blood.
20. That I really don't sing as good as I think I do, but I should still sing anyway.
21. That the mother is always the glue that holds a family together.
22. To always be a hard worker.
23. That blueberries in heavy cream, although fattening, is amazing.
24. How to bargain shop.
25. That cancer f'in sucks.
26. That I couldn't have asked for a better mom.
27. That no one really cares if I wear white after Labor Day.
28. To never take a drink from a stranger.
29. That no matter how old I am, she would always worry about me.
30. That angels really are real.
31. And the most important thing I've ever learned from my mother is that love has no boundaries or limits and even after someone dies, their love does not die with them.

I encourage you to make a list of 31 things your mother taught you.

1. _____

   _____

2. _____

   _____

3. _____

   _____

4. _____

   _____

5. _____

   _____

6. _____

   _____

7. _____

_____

8. _____

_____

9. _____

_____

10. _____

_____

11. _____

_____

12. _____

_____

13. _____

_____

14. _____

_____

15. _____

_____

16. _____

_____

17. _____

_____

18. _____

_____

19. _____

_____

20. _____

_____

21. _____

_____

22. _____

_____

23. _____

_____

24. _____

_____

25. _____

_____

26. _____

_____

27. _____

_____

28. _____

_____

29. _____

_____

30. _____

_____

31. _____

_____

THE THINGS I MISS THE MOST

I miss her laugh. My mom was always laughing about something, but there are moments I remember, little inside jokes between her and I, and when I think of them I can hear her uncontrollable laugh. I would give anything to have one last laugh with her.

I miss her spaghetti and meat balls, I miss her homemade chicken soup, and I miss her telling me I eat way too fast. My mom made the best spaghetti and meatballs. Even after having chemotherapy she would be sure to have that homemade meal on the table for us all every Sunday. She would always tell me that I eat way to fast and if I didn't slow down I would choke. I always got a kick out of her saying that.

I miss her calling me way too much. I don't think a day went by that I didn't talk to my mom at least 5 times a day. Sometimes she would call a little too much, but it's funny how one day when the phone stops ringing, you'd give up your whole life to hear it ring again.

I miss how much she worried about me. She worried about me every second of every day. And I am certain that no matter what my age she would have continued to carry that same worry.

I miss her hand on my forehead when I said I wasn't feeling well. The minute I would say I didn't feel well my mom would take the back of her hand and place it on my forehead to check if I had a fever. I miss her touch and I miss the way she took care of me.

I miss playing "name that tune" when we were in the car together. We would put the radio on scan and let it go, the first one to scream out the correct song and artist would get a point. We both loved music and loved that game.

I miss her missing me. When I moved out on my own she would always try to get me to come over even if she had to bribe me, she always wanted me and my sister at her house and nothing made her happier than our family all together.

I miss her raspy voice. Just like mine. I have one voicemail with her voice on it and as hard as it is for me to listen to I sometimes force myself to simply because I don't ever want to forget the sound of her voice.

I miss her horrible spelling and grammar. She was the worst with spelling and grammar but it was so incredibly cute. She would always post positive things on Facebook (which so many people loved) half of the time the spelling was way off but the message of positivity was so clear and I loved that.

I miss her passion for the people she loved. All my mom ever wanted in life was to spend as much time with her family and close friends as possible. She was so simple. Cancer robbed her from it all but the love she has for all of us was enough for a lifetime.

I miss her beautiful photography. She took some beautiful photos as she was in the stages of learning photography. It breaks my heart that she didn't get to continue on her dream. I miss taking her to chemotherapy. Never in a million years did I think I would hear myself say that. I never wanted to have to take my beautiful, young, full-of-life mom to chemo. But the day came when I had to and it became a routine every 3rd Friday we would go together and sit there for 4+ hours. She made friends in there, she made people laugh in there and I would give up every day for the rest of my life to be able to sit there with her again.

I miss her love. I am surrounded by people every day, people who love and care about me more than I think, but no body, and I mean nobody will ever love me the way my mom did and that void of missing her will never, ever be filled.

What are some of the things that you miss the most about your mom?

WHAT YOU SEE IN THE WORLD AROUND YOU

I often look back at particular events in life and wonder if certain people are placed into your life for a reason, if certain things happen to prepare you for what's to come. Once you are born, is your life already entirely planned out for you? Can you really fight fate or is everything just one big coincidence?

I truly believe that what you see in the world around you is a reflection of who you are. Positivity plays a big part in life. You can spend life feeling sorry for yourself for unfortunate burdens that have come your way, or you can collect yourself and move on. Move on to be a stronger person, a better person, a person that you would want to know.

The past can't be changed nor is it made to be. You cannot dwell on what already has come and gone, but you can control how you will your future will turn out. You can control it with a certain mind set, you must set yourself up for the worst, so when the worst comes you're prepared. But never give up on hope.

I think we sometimes get so caught up in lives busy moments that we forget to stop and think about the simple things. The phone calls to an old friend, telling someone how much you truly love them and the simple walks around your neighborhood. I don't think we forget about these moments on purpose, I just think we assume these moments and opportunities will never be taken away. This is why we must walk slower, open our eyes so we don't miss all the great things that are passing by.

There are days I feel that I have lost my way, I get off track of where I want to be but I force myself to find the strength to keep on going, just like my mom did before she passed away. Though she is no longer physically here on earth, I do believe that she sends me strength. The same strength she used to hide her pain, the same strength she used to make others smile even while her own heart was breaking, and for me that is an irreplaceable gift that she has given me, and it could never be taken away.

THROUGH THE EYES OF A BEST FRIEND

Written by Joelle Sutera

"I'll never forget the day when I got that call. I was on the phone with my best friend Jenna when she was driving over to her parents' house to find out the news that her mother had just received from the doctor. We are both very optimistic and light hearted so we never expected to hear the news that we heard on that sad day. She arrived at her parents' house and told me she would call me back when she was leaving. I don't even think ten minutes went by when she called me back in a screaming panic, yelling that her mother had Stage Four Lung Cancer. I didn't know what to do or what to say. I was in shock. I have never had anyone that close to me be that ill nor was I that great at dealing with this kind of stuff. I did know that from that point forward I had one job to do and that job was to be there for her. That's all I could do was be there. When she wanted to cry, when she wanted to talk, or even when she simply just wanted to have someone to sit there in silence with, I knew I had to be that person for her.

Those next few months were a roller coaster ride for everyone. Her mom had some great days along with some bad days as well but the greatest day that I can remember was about a month before her mom had passed away.

Gina, Jenna's mom, was feeling really awesome so we all decided to go to the casino to gamble, have some drinks, and eat some crab legs. We shared lots and lots of laughs. We took a ton of pictures and the happiness shown on both of their faces was incredible. I will never forget that day.

Still through all of this, the positivity was never out of site. It was amazing. Not long after that amazing day that we had all spent together, Gina became our guardian angel.

Flash back to our friendship that started when we were just nine years old. We had a rocky patch in high school as all immature teenagers do but at 18 years old we were lucky enough to find each other again and we immediately picked up right where we had left off, almost as if time hadn't even passed at all.

Ever since the day I met Jenna she has always been such a strong person, one of the strongest people I know as a matter of fact. I don't know if she knows this about our friendship but her strength was something I had always admired about her. She doesn't sweat the small stuff and she sees the good in everyone life brings her way. She wakes up every day with a smile ready to face the day. The most amazing thing about her strength is that it just got even stronger after the passing of her mother. She got even better at seeing the best in people, always giving them the benefit of the doubt because she knew first hand that having a bad hair day was in no comparison to the tragedy that she has gone through.

So here we are almost four years later, both 27 years old and there is not a day that goes by I don't think of her mom.

In a crazy way I would say that my best friend had become an even better person after losing her mom. She has a higher appreciation of life and the small things it provides her on a daily basis. She doesn't get mad over stupid things because she knows it's simply just not worth it. She loves her friends and family more than anything.

She continues to inspire me as a person and more importantly, as a friend. People constantly ask me "How is Jenna doing with everything?" Or "You're her best friend, how is she coping?" The truth is that it feels as if sometimes her mom is still here on earth. Jenna keeps her mom's spirit alive every single day and I know that she will continue to do that for the rest of her life.

Gina's flame will burn for all of eternity all because of a daughter who wanted the world to know how incredible her mother was."

WHILE THE TIME PASSES

Before my mom was diagnosed I couldn't say I was the best person I could be. I wasn't always kind to others and I wasn't always a positive person. I truly believe that even through the worst part of my life, losing her, I started to become the amazing person she was. I found an inner strength to go on. A new reason to live life, the life that she loved to live so very much. The reason was her. All she ever wanted was for me to be happy. So that's what I was going to do.

My mission was to fulfill her wish and make sure I always did what made me happy. If it weren't for cancer I would say I have the perfect life… then again if it weren't for cancer, would I even realize it? Probably not. I would probably still be that selfish 23 year old I was before she was diagnosed.

They say time heals all wounds, but I don't believe that to be true. I believe that time has a way of making you forget, and time has a way of moving so fast that you have no choice but to go on, but some wounds will never be fully healed. Especially the ones that leave you with a broken heart and at the end of the day it is what you do while the time passes that will make all the difference…

Make your time count.

ABOUT THE AUTHOR

Jenna Rose Lowthert is 27 years old and from Roxbury, New Jersey. Jenna wrote her first book titled "Life Goes On..?" in just seven short days. She was inspired by her 48 year old mother who passed away on May 27th, 2013 after her ten month battle with Stage Four Lung Cancer. Jenna wrote this book with the intent to inspire other to find a way stitch the pieces of their broken heart back together so they can learn to live again.